TALK INTO THE LATE

by the same poet:

A Voyage Round the Moon (Peterloo Poets, 1985)
A Letter from Lewis Chaucer (Perdix Press, 1985)
A Lecturing Life (Grammelot Press, 1986)
Terra Damnata (The Dodman Press, 1988)
Hobbes's Whale (Paulinus Press, 1988)
An Incident in the Plaza del Zocodover, Toledo 1584
(Bullnettle Press, 1989)

forthcoming:
Life of Merlin (Bullnettle Press, 1993)

Talk into the Late Evening

JOHN GOHORRY

PETERLOO POETS

First published in 1992
by Peterloo Poets
2 Kelly Gardens, Calstock, Cornwall PL18 9SA, U.K.

**A catalogue record for this book is available
from the British Library**

ISBN 1-871471-26-5

Printed in Great Britain by
Latimer Trend & Company Ltd, Plymouth

ACKNOWLEDGEMENTS are due to *Encounter, The Literary Review, London Magazine, Taurus Press, The Times Literary Supplement,* and *Wind of Change* (Toronto), who first published individual poems collected here.

Several poems in this collection have been broadcast on *Poetry Now* (BBC Radio 3).

'For Breughel's Notebook', 'The True Story of Francisco de la Vega', 'On the Birkenkopf', 'Sitting in the Rosengarten', and 'From Burgberg: an Ars Poetica' are reprinted with permission from *The World & I* magazine, a publication of *The Washington Times* Corporation.

Acknowledgements are also due to the following private presses:

The Dodman Press for *Terra Damnata* (1987)
Paulinus Press for *Hobbes's Whale* (1988)
Bullnettle Press for *An Incident in the Plaza del Zocodover, Toledo 1584* (1989).

Supported by

Cornwall
County Council

For Gerlinde

Contents

Unidentified Aliens, New Mexico, 1947

They found them a couple of miles off the disc-wreckage,
still in their time-harnesses, but unbelievably aged;
their fat, scaly tongues like the tongues of chameleons
petrified by the desert heat and turned macaw perches,

and their eyestrings drawn out by desperate hummingbirds
tangled around their white mouths like failed parachutes.
Cursing the heat in their respirators they cut them free,
and stowed them like war casualties in canvas body-bags

on the floor of the gunship. Heading for Walker Field
and the Lieutenant's report to his General, Base H.Q.,
they were already naming them—Toadsucker, Silverskin,
Big Mouth, Horny White Eye, recognising them as their
  own,

and recalling too how, as they pulled Horny White Eye up
from the body heap, his hands were tight around Silverskin
as if they'd been sitting side by side in the bucketseats
at the movies, and he knew how the last reel would end.

Under Mount Fuji

Under Mount Fuji, the dayshift venerate Protocols
of Manufacturing Automation as Dr Ichikawa rehearses
the names of the Six Accomplishments—writing; archery,
music, arithmetic. Etiquette. Riding. Dr Tsukuba recalls

how the Eight Calamities bind themselves into four pairs
—grief, pain; joy, pleasure; curiosity, spying; in-breathing,
out-breathing; such elegant binary couplings. The
    clean-room
is at least free of calamities, as of particles, until today

VS/PB 20, fifth generation Matsushita out of Westinghouse,
gripped Dr Hanshawa impassively in jointed hydraulic arms
and squeezed him in two. This was a dust-controlled
    morning;
no freak electromagnetic wave booted him up to this
    atrocity,

nor was it downloaded onto him in accustomed hex; nobody
    wrote
it out for his better recall in the hiragana. Dr Ichikawa
rightly considers this an infringement of Etiquette. Dr
    Tsukuba
links pain, spying; joy, curiosity; pleasure, out-breathing.

A Garden Astronomer

His telescope, gimbal-mounted, skirts lilac bushes,
washing lines, and a neighbour's obstinate pear-tree
still blocking the night sky with its ponderous lineaments
and, every autumn, its multiple, hanging, green globes.

His evening delights are to transcend the immediate
fragrances, noise of the garden, and to reach out instead
for deodorised silence—touch the cold, sailing Moon,
in her inverted transits, Venus' clouds, Saturn's rings,

and the galaxy's distant quicksands, all silver and gold;
indoors, he watches *The Sky at Night,* writes polite letters
in a tidy, methodical hand to Patrick Moore. His
    photographs
of Kohoutek and Encke grace stairwell and dining room
    wall.

His wife, tying back their delphiniums and Pampas grasses,
is certain we are not alone, though light-years distant
from some Intelligence cocking an eye to a similar lens
in a presumed galaxy somewhere, comforted by the same
    things.

At the Alpsee: an Ars Amatoria

The girls step out of the water into the evening sunshine
their slim bodies showering light and white watersparks;
they have swum all the way from lake centre to grass edge
where proprietors sunbathing in deckchairs fondle dogs' ears

and the rich boys with black bodyhair and gold medallions
contrive *Gentlemen-starts* ostentatiously on the sandway.
They vanish into extravagant, rough towels, teeth chattering.
On the landing stage stretching right out into the lake

a brown woman of twenty-five oils her breasts with sunblock;
the low sunlight burns her skin copper; she glistens before
all the racing boys, whom she lures with her frank nakedness
and shrill accents of mockery. They jostle each other loudly

until Black Bodyhair puts one arm to her shoulder, strokes
the other behind her knees, and heaves her high, squealing,
delectable, and blissfully grappling him into the cool water.
They fall into their ecstasy, their great shrieking splash.

The girls struggle from their towels into warm cardigans;
the dog-lovers' hands are a frenzy of fur coats and hot ears.
By the landing-stage, heads bob and bodies close, playfully.
Behind them, the evening train curves towards Oberstaufen.

Sitting in the Rosengarten

The old woman has carefully folded her dog in two,
his PVC whiskers secured, waterproof ears neatly packed
in their buttondown polythene stowaway—it will not rain
this morning, anywhere in the rosegarden. Herr Dollmeyer,

stifling but immaculate in a dark worsted three-piece suit,
imagines that she is puzzled by the incongruity. Why on
    earth
should he be wearing a waistcoat, a thick silver watch chain,
and heavy, black shoes? Why this folded white handkerchief?

A courteous waitress brings coffee, vanilla ice creams;
they bloom with unusual fragrance this year, the red roses,
as they bloomed in her grandparents' garden in Breslau
in the summer of '35. *Liegt in der Tschechoslovakei, net . . . ?*

Mothers pass by on their way to and from the Liszthalle
grussgotting and gutentaging one another in civil exchanges;
Herr Dollmeyer imagines funerals, long-service presentations,
bouquets of heady roses in cellophane, printed name-cards.

The old woman's brother, before he died, would wander
    about
randomly, at a great age, all over the city. He would ring
doorbells to strange apartments he mistook for his own
    home,
pick roses out of the park, donate them to bemused women.

Visiting Schorndorf

A man in a stove-pipe hat stood, unregarded,
in Main Street at twelve noon that winter Friday;
light snow was falling, the air sharp with pine frost,
pastel frescoes of saints and black frakturschrift

ribbonning over the pink end-wall of the Bäckerei
where icicles hung in the brittle beauty of glass.
From some upstairs window a Bach Violin Sonata danced
its way out into the street, a *perpetuum mobile* sawing

time into a thousand fractalled replicas of itself
while space turned to latticework, measured intervals
merely, between snowflake and snowflake. Dr Allmeyer
sat in a shiny leather armchair, his surgery empty,

and surrendered his griefs to the *perpetuum mobile;*
the customers in the baker's, buying their brötchen,
heard it, too, trading silver coin for the hot loaves,
and the man in the stove-pipe hat shuffled his galoshes

into hardly visible dance steps, the snow lying scuffed
where he turned his toes outwards. On the down platform
two men in thick overcoats and navy blue woollen gloves
posed in grotesque attitudes, pretending to be trees.

From Burgberg: an Ars Poetica

(i) *Show*

The ravine discloses itself discreetly to sedate families
on the restaurant balcony overlooking the Starzlachklamm;
but the teenagers have discovered a precipice at its margin

just safe enough to slide shrieking down, into the icy cascade
and at its foot the blue bowl which the forest shade hangs
    over.
Time is a sundial's gloss: *Horam monstro quam tibi dedit Deus.*

(ii) *Name*

Everywhere, there is white and green land. The sky has its
    peaks
touched by the naming imagination—Kratzer, Trettach
    Mädelgabel,
Hochfrottspitze; Bockkarkopf, Steinschartenkopf, Hohes
    Licht —

their granite distinguished, brought into the compass of
    diners
and fathers exploring their rocky ways with teenage children;
one step at a time we understand one another, apprehend
    new names.

(iii) *Illuminate*

Against glass, at the back of the balcony fresh now after
    rain,
set the stained-glass Christmas lights, kite, schooner, and
    globes;
set them spinning in the graceful turns of an evening
    Lichtspiel

so that the yellow and crimson flares urge their peculiar
    flames
round and round on our inner walls, and we ourselves
    become changed
—magic creatures of glass; mountain light falling; a dance
    visible.

Pictures from Hannover

Outside the Hauptbahnhof, the old king steadies his
   war-horse,
its nostrils funnelling smoke into the soft, penetrant drizzle.
His head and his sword are uplifted, eyes levelled at C & A.

In the Kaufhof, you can ransom a leather football for
   DM 25
but the fox furs are prisoners wired to electronic alarms
—offer them freedom, and the universe shrieks accusations.

The Passerelle is a football pitch where teenage Gerd
   Müllers
exhibit their dazzling footwork, crackling first-time volleys
into the back of the gift-shop. The Gunners are playing at
   home.

The Zirkus Roncalli present a new sad clown—the true heir,
everyone says, of Grock and Grimaldi. While you are
   watching him
a three year old child takes your hand calmly, does not let
   go.

The precincts are heavy with buskers, beggars,
   organ-grinders,
and two stout Churchillian figures with drowning umbrellas;
the real city could be a mirror for all conditions of man.

Certain Events in Kitteldorf

They went off in the morning at a sharp hour, shouldering
canvas bags covering airguns and coarse fishing tackle,
their thick-soled rubber boots clumping over the bridge
where the Neckar in flood ran over her ancient songs;
early risers at breakfast in the Old Mill watched them go,
vanishing into oblique mist, their forgotten vocabularies.
The day organised itself methodically into a steady drizzle.
You'll see, said the proprietor, straight out of Tuscaloosa;

they'll be back tonight full of tall stories, drunk as skunks.
Their expedition was a straggle of gunshot, of groundbait
wistfully broadcast, rubber boots skidding over the bracken.
That night, the Teubners were dining out at the Old Mill,
—a celebration feast for their Golden Wedding Anniversary.
Herr Teubner, wineglass in hand, spoke of accumulations,
of lives running their course downstream, carrying sediment
through channels scoured deeper each season onto the
    bedrock

until here at last were the still waters, dark and brooding,
into which people might cast for a fish, for a wise word.
Applause, then, and resumed celebrations—waiters scurrying
attentively to the tables, toasts, stories and anecdotes,
reminiscences, teasings and wooings—the whole restaurant
bright with civilised noises, conversation and laughter.
Until, at about ten, there were the sounds of a disturbance
—shouts, raucous songbursts from the direction of the
    bridge.

They strode in through the doorway, mud on their rubber
    boots,
fish kissing their wrists in limp, silver shoals, their waists
trussed with brown ears, fur swinging below. The air reeked
of gunbarrels, whisky, rude manliness. They stumbled among
the stained tablecloths, lurched towards ringing interiors.
The Teubners addressed themselves to the unfinished
    discourse,
as was proper. *Everything is proper*, murmured Herr Teubner.
Then paused—*But the Arse does belong inside the Trousers.*

17

Geistliches Lied

All that remains now is air set in motion,
the reverberant marching vigour of the motet
Übers Gebirg Maria geht, each footstep pacing
towards the everyday rapture of a magnificat.

The great spire of the Minster is hands praying,
ornate Gothic icing on The Bride's wedding cake;
on the Rathaus facade the frescoes gesticulate
at the Danube, where history is an opaque

mirror crowded with pleasureboats while my stylus
here in this other place is a rocksteady monitor
of voices astride your music, John Eccard, like cyclists
who endlessly overhaul, slipstream and project one another

into imagined space. From the top of the spire
I can see, ninety leagues northwards, the Magdeburg road
out of Mühlhausen, over the Harz mountains,
and on it twelve disciplined cyclists pedalling hard

past a plain country girl sent from her father's shack
out in the pine forests to do menial errands;
their breath huffs out foreshortened *Hail Marys*
jocosely in white clouds familiar as her old friends.

On the Birkenkopf

For five years they steadily carried it up itself
with diggers, bulldozers, and mechanical shovels
—tipped it out by the bucketful, by the lorryload,
either side of the winding trackway their huge wheels

pressed out of the earthwork, compacting the uprise
with steamrollers, pneumatic hammers. Millions
of cubic metres of lintels, cornices, door-jambs
tumbled out in a cascade of thumping hydraulics

as the city cleared of its rubble, the trackway rose,
and saplings already took root in the lower slopes
of the conceived mountain. We walk up to the summit
tonight, crossing through forty years' woodland—

shrubs sprawl in profusion, greenery hangs everywhere
over the weedy path, and the sun flames itself down
in magnificent splendour past Renningen; beacon lights
from the Fernsehturm scour the hills rhythmically

and the winking city below us is dancing, suspended
it seems, in mid-air. Hölderlin's evening sky blooms
in the fragrance of dog roses and wild honeysuckle,
the gigantic, collapsed colonnades of a ruined garden

seeding themselves, bombed houses exfoliating debris
—porch, windowsill, gate-arch, shattered mantelpiece,
relics weathered by time and our plain determination
to build high, high into the air, and not to forget.

We turn from the summit, guessing at the deep centre.
My grandfather pulled wood from the blitzed cathedral
and had candlesticks fashioned from it; small comforts
he said, and to keep darkness from having the last word.

At Middle Aston

They fly over his park at night, the owl widows,
hooting and shrieking above the lake in great swarms,
their ghostly feathers sudden in the white moonshine;
they are clouds among those trees still in mourning.

He hanged them for small trespasses, their husbands
—stealing sheep, two bushels of barley, loaves of bread;
they lay in the coverts, half-clothed and desperate,
their sacks lagged with coarse string, only their need warm.

His mercy was transportation, his property fenced about
with the thick stakes they whittled for boundary-work.
On the wide lake his birds float stiffly, like decoys;
his carp turn to stone passing under the old gibbet.

At an Airbase Perimeter

The hawks soar, scream and wheel over the valley-floor,
their flight-path illuminated by neatly ranged blood-oranges;
the clouds in which they lie concealed squeal in pain,
and sound itself lags behind them, fearfully dislocated.

What pleasure their brooding knows melts into the hill,
its ecstasies guessed at from the even, retracted runways;
omniscience is their radar-eye, their fresh-plotted domain
the anxiety of the new bride, the terrified child's nightmare.

Their grandparents hatched monsters, anencephalous
    minotaurs
and the one they called Big Boy that burned shadows solid;
they are nesting again, roosting each year more familiarly,
more terrible every spring their welcome, obscene cries.

Musicians Rehearsing al fresco

They hold down their music with plastic clothes-pegs
(the light, April wind blustering *adagio assai*
over the paddock where newly-born lambs are grazing);
First Violin flicks blossom from his Cremona fiddle

with birthday-cake fingers, while Fräulein D'Amore
picks out *In an English Country Garden, a tempo giusto*,
on her viola. Madame Svoboda curses the barbed wire
that threatens her cellocase, and measures the horsehair

of her second-best bow against some bayard strands
caught on the fence-snaggings. From the milking sheds
rise the clatter of harpsichords and a flute trilling
and falling, the first flutter of conversations

between brass and woodwind. The Violins, grown impatient,
exchange glances, rapping music stands. The Estate trees
flurry, and heave to attention. The bows drop in fury.
They savage the notes off the stave, like mad dogs.

Acker Bilk in Concert

Their snazzy silk waistcoats are gaudy as deckchairs
set fluttering all the way along the striped sand
as the New Hippodrome Management proudly presents
Mr Acker Bilk and his Paramount Jazz Band

—on whose sleeve notes Teutonic upper-case Incipits
augment a diction that's pure Brobdingnag Aureate:-
Herein the Ensemble's Titular Head executes
Effusions so far Unparalleled upon the Clarionett.

But nothing's distorted tonight as *Tiger Rag*
thumps its way out under the stuccoed awning
of the proscenium, where bright blue birds hover
and the rock solid cliffs of Dover will hit morning

into a cocked hat, a bowler hat, or any God
-blessed hat that you like, up as high as your top C;
in the meantime *Let it shine, Oh good Lord let it shine*
let the light from that lighthouse shine on me!

Now into the pit and the stalls ranges his raw blues;
Dardanella, a cold shiver under the sunshades;
the beach is a desolate sidewalk where over-leafed
gangsters sit cautiously sipping iced lemonades.

Time chastens us all, band, gangsters, fat usherettes
wading awkwardly out to sea for the rowdy encore
—which is the Hippodrome Manager crossing the bar
fifty years hence, still whistling *Stranger on the Shore*.

Vivaldi, No. 3 Lab, 1958

He took off his clothes and climbed into the fume cupboard,
the strings already launched into their bright *Allegro*;
mother-naked among clamps, carboys and adjustable stands
he squatted, homunculus in a glass case, a man in a bottle.

The organpipes that were bunsen burners crackled and sang;
wharrup wharrup the flames drummed and the air burned with
a green glow of volcanoes. Harpsichords in a low register
thumped and clattered about on the far edges of harmony.

Over beside the balance room the beautiful Miss Kodalskaya
carefully dropped universal indicator into a glass beaker;
her steady blue eyes measured titrations. Light condensed,
and the glass beaker suddenly clouded. Nothing was said.

A Letter from Thomas Love Peacock

Sheldrop's the perfect host. Lightly grilled turbot
for breakfast this morning, and sauteed mushrooms,
a particular favourite of mine, although Jaquinetta,
of course, prefers prunes. Claret flows in abundance;
at dinner yesterday we drank some distinguished Pomerols
and afterwards half a dozen bottles of fine Madeira.

The house is called Grimstone Gables; etymology suggests
a forbidding appearance, or perhaps fabric weathered
over the years with soot and grime. My own inclination
is towards Grimm, otherwise Grjmma, eponymous founder
of a settlement hereabouts in the time of King Ethelred.
We are well off for entertainments; the lawns are extensive

and there are some fine prospects—an arboretum, a folly.
Quinetta and I walked this morning to the Palladian temple,
fed goldfish, and then made our way back to the orangery.
There is a landing stage on the river and a skiff moored
ready for outings. Sheldrop has become very keen on rowing;
he is developing an interesting theory of muscular rhythms.

The library's first rate—Banks' *Florilegium*, Metastasio,
and *The Red Book of Hergest* alongside Homer and Plutarch
—everyone you could wish to engage with. I've been looking
at patented systems for a geometrical method of learning
to fence, following patterns marked out on a plain floor.
Sheldrop and I are experimenting tomorrow in slow motion.

Best of all are the conversations. Mrs Magdalen Sheldrop,
whose condition you know of, arraigned young Dr
    Craniarch,
the logician, all yesterday evening, on supernatural beings.
Miss Clarinda sings lullabies and debates Excluded Middles
with considerable acumen. Quinetta has taken up drawing.
Write when you can. There is stuff here good for fiction.

The Bracelet

Now that she blushed with pleasure whenever
he called on her, he knew that she was ready
for declarations. What should she be waiting for?
He could assert now that they would be going steady.

Now he allowed her to know he remembered
the dress she had worn a week back and her face
flushed with gratitude, he knew that the time had come;
he had mastered her, seeing now that she knew her place.

He knew now for a certainty that he controlled
her, and would do so forseeably, without any risk
of rejection or petulant questioning. So he
unclipped the thick silver chain with its bright disc

and, with a proud smile, hung it around her arm.
She swooned, as was obligatory. Her one regret
unexpressed in the ecstasy of this performed minute
would eventually drive her from him. Though not yet

as she hung on him, ostentatiously, like the bracelet.

The Marine Aquarium, Penzance

We mime our way awkwardly into the half-darkness
of the municipal aquarium, our eyes accommodating
to a dumb world of gills fanning and suspended gravels;

already our thoughts are eddying up in cartoon-bubbles
past the great conger, his nose buried among the rocks,
and the stately sea bass, their scales hall-marked

with mother-of-pearl insignia. They glide in echelons,
their symmetry the perfection of rehearsed manoeuvres
or an instinct at one with its waters, frosty as arctic

depicted in iceberg blues on the back panel. We rely
on the tank placards to name for us the breathing sand
where a turbot conforms to our idea of itself, almost

invisible, and other fish press into annihilations,
the flattened, amorous virtuosi of the low profile.
Cold, ultramarine. The lobster performs his slow dance

straight out of *Alice in Wonderland*, kissing to death
under the rock-stack; the crayfish spreads herself wide,
gathering space, the huge, vaulted reach between water

and water. The aquarium folds into itself at the exit.
Where the conger swallows his tail and daylight is again
a routine, dizzy clamour, we burst back into our language.

À Place Determinate

Sometimes a man knows a place determinate, within the compass whereof he is to seek;
and then his thoughts run over all the parts thereof, in the same manner as one would
sweep a room to find a jewel; or as a spaniel ranges the field, till he find a scent, or as
a man should run over the alphabet, to start a rhyme ...
(Hobbes, *Leviathan* Part 1 Cap 3)

What were the girls doing, tying up their hair
in the garage, eyeshadow and blusher discarded
among fuse-wire and toolboxes? And a gold ear-ring
gone missing now, somewhere among the oilstains
and the dahlia corms sprinkled with sulphur!

And for what word do we suppose Towser was hunting,
his wet nose mauling *Wyld's Etymological Dictionary*
somewhere between *Bl-* and *Br-*? The old cynics
said that any dog with a good nose for a scent
was a past master of the disjunctive syllogism.

Fetch the broom, Jonah; we'll sweep for the jewel,
take the dog for a walk through the daisyfields
and drive the composed girls out to their engagement
in great style. Then afterwards, we'll scrutinise
alphabets over at your place, and etymologise.

Joker

He harbours them all—the cowboys in paper trousers,
the Irish shoe-thief and the ten stone budgerigar,
the naive girl who mistakes China's capital,
and the raincoated nobody hailed in St Peter's Square,
bringing them out to narrate their rehearsed histories
like old friends in the canteen or the corridor,
preposterous agents in perfectly normal settings
—costive owls, organgrinders, giraffes in a public bar.

The true chronicler of their exploits embroiders, perhaps,
but only to free his listeners from the stupor
of literal attachment to fact, or the routine glaze
that accompanies the regular reading of any newspaper.
He comes to you not with the bold banner headline
for solicitors struck off the Rolls or the pilot's chopper
but an explosive punch or a pun to insinuate
that underneath, every accepted notion is quite improper.

Except of course that we are all like the absurd Irishman
escaping in one Wellington boot and a high heel
from the posse of circumstances that will harry us
to a grave that is painfully funny and quite real.
And the joker himself, in raincoat and paper trousers,
is wondering all along just how it will feel
to be struck by the thunderbolt, like the wrong golfer,
or dished up to the budgerigar as a square meal.

Talk into the Late Evening

They are slowly falling asleep at last in the wicker nursery,
bears, blossoms and comforters strewn over their
   counterpanes
while the inexhaustible summer sunlight still improvises a
   dance

through the appletrees, and their curtains turn distant lands
hailed through the yellow roomshine by their explorers'
   vowels;
Cra-croucrou, they are calling, *toohou, cacrou, toutou, toohou.*

Downstairs, there are bright adult sallies of arrival and
   greeting
—laughter—*Oh, those magnificent flowers! Fetch a vase, darling!*
bubbles the hostess, then—*What a beautiful dress you are
   wearing!*

from the fragrant male guests fluttering to her candle flame.
And later, when wineglasses are emptied and cutlery clatters
over the smoothed tablecloth, there is the stridor of small
   talk

growing more serious until night thickens in the laurel bushes
and the dinner party projects itself through the open
   windows
in a corona of yellow light out onto the fold-aways of the
   lawn.

Upstairs, the far countries have slipped into a short silence;
but making their goodnight calls at the gate under a white
   moon
they keep an ear open for new languages, slowly becoming
   theirs.

Charade

It is either an early retirement or a long-service award
for the Word Manager this morning at 7a.m.;
he is supine, still crashed out from the night before,
still sleeping it off under the continental quilt
with the Food Manager in her black nightdress.
The M.D. comes over in his towelling stretch-suit,
a moon and stars embroidered above the left breast,
to flourish awards from the side-table. *Glasses*
he booms, and then *Clock* in stentorian fashion,
leaning over the Food Manager to make the presentation.

The recipient gratefully straps on the black wristwatch,
pokes the spectacles onto his nose, smiles, lost for words.
Downstairs the M.D. wants his garage and best cars
arranged properly on the plastic tray. *Civilisation*
he shouts. The Word Manager sneezes hard; the Deputy
    M.D.
bursts into tears at this sudden explosion. The Food Manager
positions the Rolls and the D.B.7 by the open doors
of the red garage. The M.D. selects one. *Civilisation*
he bellows again, and then *When the saints go marching in*.
The Rolls and the D.B.7 glide through the blue doorways.

Hobbes's Whale

'In a good poem, whether it be *epic*, or *dramatic;* as also in *sonnets, epigrams*
and other pieces, both judgement and fancy are required: but the fancy
must be eminent, because they please for the extravagancy; but ought not
to displease by indiscretion.'
Hobbes, *Leviathan* 1 viii (Of the Virtues Commonly called Intellectual; and
their Contrary Defects)

1. A NATIVITY IN WESTPORT

A bad night, surely, with her husband in quarrel
run off to London, and never like to return;
and now Cousin Francis comes all flushes and short breath
with fresh news out of Weymouth not two days old

of six great Spanish terror ships full of cannon
and black letter Madrid Bibles billying up the Channel,
the torturers' vanguard full-rigged, making good headway.
She tumbles onto the rushes, her own blood burdened,

and even that great linen swathe under her heart
taut with its own small apprehensions belike
bunched in *hysterica passio*. Seven fattening months
she has borne him, like some vigilant Nordcaper,

but these travails will beach him tonight ready or no.
The midwife is summoned with towels and the secret lore
of innermost chambers, for already the hours squeeze,
tighten, and press her; how else shall she be delivered?

The night promises, threatens, but evades questioning
in rehearsed Spanish manoeuvres that terrify, suffocate
with tightly clenched hands and Jesuitical enigmas;
upstairs, Cousin Francis drowses beside a low candle,

as Beldame spits on her hands and Mistress Anne labours,
their voices in prayer making hastily-drawn prologues
to this crying text which even as daylight breaks
nudges himself towards print. Now comes deliverance

with a shriek, her fresh boy cast out onto the sheet
all seaspray, all salt. She holds him, whispering comfort.
Cousin Francis brings *rosa solis* and oatcake; Weymouth news
is of ghostships, lucid skies, daylight, terror appeased.

2. WATERSONG

Now he has language, she names the toy ships for him,
wooden splints launched into the currents of Back Brook
—the *Tamberlane, Easterband,* and the *Tiny So Tiny*
proud in their galleon finery, leaf sails all billowing

as they glide from their sheltered Cadiz into the main
        channel
of her coaxing *Come all ye's,* to be eddied in whirlpools,
sounded down to drowned river-gravels, or thrown headlong
onto those boulder reefs, that providential, speaking white
        foam.

Downstream on the hoe, her muddy boys juggle their jacks
up from the bowling-green floor onto the back of the hand
and into vanishing palms, one eye on the bobbing fleet
that advances, already disconsolate, in louring weather

to their promontory. They crawl to the ness edge, hurling
clods, pebbles and flints at the bucking flotilla,
its capitanas spreadeagled athwart the supposed dyke floods,
their imagined black sails reefed into their own mourning.

The burst water swallows the ships in its sibilant echoes,
their waterlogged vowels submerged, the boys' treble *Hurrahs*
piping in and out of the brook noise, the just sea-clamour.
He will never forget her laughter, her hands suddenly cold.

3. MR LATIMER'S TRIVIUM

They have spread out their damp sheets on the bleaching-
    green,
Gammer Rosewood and all the young wives, tolerant as
    usual
of the pedagogue Mr Latimer, *an excellent Graecian Greek
scholar,*
who has today brought his pupils out into the fresh air, slates

and books bound in their old parchments also spread on the
    green
for construing his homily. The boys struggle hard with the
    text
They that observe lying vanities forsake their own mercy,
his diligent exposition as fugitive as their own aspirations

in this mid-morning sunshine, only Corvus, it seems,
    comprehending
the exact thrust of his suasorium. An abrupt interrogative
sunders the joined drone of bees and the Fourth Declension
—'*Quid tu scribes, o Corve, mi fili? Mi Corve, monstra mihi!*'

Gammer Rosewood, over the green, halts in mid-anecdote;
    boys
find that elusive caesura placed between terror and mirth
as The Crow trails to the desk, manuscript book in one hand
and in the other a fat quarto. '*En Euripides!*' his voice at once

kindly—'*rogo ut explices.*'
                                   '*Ea quae Graece legebam, o magister,
Latine reddebam.*' From the old drama of the butchered
    children
he reads a verse: 'Θυμος δε κρεισσων τον εμων βουλεματων
οσπερ μεγιστων αιτιος κακων βροτοις. *Redde, mi Corve,
Latine.*'

Cui Corvus: *'Dementiis autem debellantur consilia severa;*
unde hominibus calamitates eheu! accident atrocissimae.' Latimer
—*'Ita est: Vanitates dementiaeque e ceto non evomebuntur:*
hoc reminendum est, optime; ex illo ore nil nisi veritatem.'

Hoc reminendum est—long after that transversed text has gone
to wrap oven pies, he will fashion from memory an entirely
    new
ennaration of the πεπλεγμενος μυθος in an unvarnished
    tongue.
Gammer Rosewood's resumed narrative blanches the spread
    sheets.

4. RESTORATIVES

After the second Earl's death, he locked himself up
in the great oaken cupboards where apples were stored

for the cidermaking and would speak to nobody until
his mulberry grief wore itself down to the flagstones

at five in the morning. Then Master Lawes came to visit,
bringing with him his best voice and an old bass viol
and the loose sheets of a new song he had quilled out
on the back of some turkeyskin—*o cete gigantice*

to the scholars—*o domine maris insula undulans*—
but to his friend, a daft ballad of a fine blue whale

washed ashore at Ancona, the beachscourers combing
her flank for fresh ambergris—a cold hearted girl

it was said, who would not exchange flesh with the man
that desired her, metamorphosed into a cold fish

by retributive Justice. Measure and burden rehearse,
distance, and pace one another among the old cidervats,

their grained oak sodden with birtle, the very floor
juicy with recollection, and some of the old joys

35

testing their foothold again under the pitched eaves
as their harmonies move to conclusion. Afterwards,

he lay alone again in his chamber, gaping on maps
still avoiding, as much as he could, to conclude hastily

—that fable of Jonah, the Matter of *cetus*, how a man
might spend three days, or three years, being trawled

through his mouthbrushes; his Artificer; how he is made;
his love and government; what sea is without whales.

5. NIGHT STUDIES

Not many books in his chamber, ever, and those
for repeated use—*Homer and Virgil, Xenophon,*
or some probable history, and Greek Testament,
or so—though, especially, for when he had gone

to bed, books of written music lying on his table
—his Tallis, his Dowland—and always, his Henry Lawes
to sing aloud (*not that he had a very good voice,*
but for his health's sake) behind securely locked doors

that he might not be overheard singing nonsense
—*In quel gelato core piagne madonna, tavola*
—*Doremi fasolati? Doti laso famiredo, soprano*
—or his Ballad of the whale washed ashore at Ancona

on Wednesday the fourscore of April last, certainly,
and of how sightseers came to see stranded Leviathan
in its death-throes, the salt air heady with ambergris
and hyperbole, the beach loud with the admiration

of thieves, horsemen, prospectors, and truant schoolboys
making up a newly-drawn probable Map of the whole State
of Mankind, which is both whale flushed from his element,
and the land creatures, short, brutish, degenerate,

hacking away at its ears. It is loosely engendered yet,
this allegory, not yet perfectly drawn, like a knife,
or a man locked away at night in his own small room
singing lustily into the small hours to prolong life.

6. EXILES

Even as they discourse, the state shakes. In the *Rue des Quatre
    Vents,*
the Fronde have built barricades, and this afternoon, musket
    shot
clatters irregularly from the west door of *St Jacques la
    Boucherie.*
How he disliked a direct wind blowing, even gently, into his
    face

while on horseback, little Godolphin, but was felled
    nonetheless
in the porch of *The Three Crowns* at Chagworth by an
    undiscerned,
undiscerning hand. And his royal highness' own present
    condition
—in exile, his father's person detained on the edge of
    checkmate—

calls for sober consideration of covenants voluntarily entered
    into
for our mutual benefit, the containment of these natural
    passions
within that argued Leviathan, the Commonwealth, which, at
    first
seeming impossible as a derived proposition of Euclid's, yet
    via

scrupulous reasoning, and a style that cleaves clamouring
  sense
to her rooted disjunctions, may be quarried to probable
  axioms
of rational obligation. There is a geometry to portray all
  human
conditions—the pyramid, monarchy; the rectangular
  parliaments

given to parallel opposition; man, too, in his noble
  proportions,
as Vitruvius showed, generating from many described
  consonances
all figures imaginable. He rotates the neatly squared graph
  paper
and traces huge tail fins arching round the figure's splayed
  feet;

a great gaping mouth from elbows to genitals, and
  protruding from it
the torso and perfectly circular head, arms widely
  spreadeagled.
His thighs are perfectly matched salmon, leaping towards the
  navel.
In the *Rue Polydore*, a horseman has been dismounted, hacked
  to death.

7. BEHEMOTH

Walking, aged eighty-seven, from the Real Tennis Courts
where he has exercised, been well rubbed by a strong
  woman,
he encounters a boisterous coterie of wits, fops, and cullies;
the Ballers, whose chief pleasures are Dame Bennett's ladies,

the destruction of glass chronometers, and bear-taunting.
They surround him, their wigs fluttering in sensual ringlets,
and goad the old baldhead—'*What destiny pricks a man fiercer
than Bishop Bramble's revenge? Why, your French bone-ache!*

What shall his prize be who has squared the circle? Nothing
but mathematical claps.' He immerses his age in their repartees
as behemoth sinks his bulk into water, eyes periscopes over
the flood, and his nostrils two heaving shafts at waterlevel.

Their wit is celerity of imagining, but unstable, quicksilver.
His is steady as ever, thoughts lumbering towards a
    certainty.
Truth is the right ordering of names in our affirmations;
he taketh it in with his eyes: his nose pierceth through snares.

8. FULL CIRCLE

It comes to him at night from one of the reed-edged ponds
on the far side of the park, its bottle-glass eye pressed
to the mullions, its resonant lung charged with ichor;

elsewhere in the room-shadows are his manuscript-sheets,
—fresh controversies limned in accordance with old habits
for exemplification, and suchlike; some geometrical Trials;

drafts of a late Amorous Verse. Of all discourse governed
by thirst for knowledge, there is at last an end—either
attainment or giving over bringing utterance to conclusion;

the nurse troubles his waking with nostrums and rose of
    solace,
lenitives for the strangury. Certainly *no discourse whatsoever*
can end in absolute knowledge of fact, past or to come,

for knowledge of fact is first, sense, and then, memory,
each with its infidelities. His lord's choir sang the Advent
Hymn *Vox clara ecce intonat* as his litter was carried out

over Umberley Sick but at last there are no clear voices;
the house trembles, is swallowed up in a submarine darkness.
On the far ponds a silence settles, after great waves.

A Letter to Lady Pecunia

Dear Lady,
    My name probably won't mean very much
to you, although I regularly keep in touch
with your champagne breakfasts and intimate suppers,
being an avid reader of the quality newspapers.

I have followed your fortunes and your affairs
devotedly—studied your portfolios of shares
and investment accounts with building societies
like a distant suitor calculating the niceties

of advantage for his remote beloved's prosperity.
I have wished you every good wish that may be.
On your birthday and at all other festivals I am
prompt with my congratulatory telegram

—your engagements, weddings, family occasions
call up my willing and anonymous donations,
and although my discreet habit has been to rejoice
for you privately, sometimes my public voice

has defended your honour, one of the dividends
Virtue can count on from having loyal friends.
So when Scandal drags your good name through his filthy
    lists
I am the first to correct gossip columnists

with irate phonecalls and strongly worded letters;
respect is the proper stance towards one's betters.
I speak always for your reputation, with regard
for your honour only, not seeking my own reward.

But recently my own finances have hit a bad patch;
I haven't a single 50 pence piece left to scratch
the back of my chequebook with, let alone piles
of notes to pay gas or electricity bills.

Every day the post brings demands for my overdue
payments, final reminders, licences to renew,
and my bank manager is a usurious tyrant
wanting his pound of flesh with every bank statement

who to ensure a large overdraft enlarges
oppresses me with account and service charges.
It's not that I am extravagant, though I overspend
—I work hard, live a moderate life, make and mend

with an old car, a few hens, a black and white TV
set, as thrifty and economical as you can be.
I do not go in for exotic holidays
in the Fortunate Isles, Manchuria, or the Canaries

but after careful scrutiny might decide
on a week in a rented caravan at the seaside.
The fact of the matter is that I have few vices
apart from the firm habit of ignoring invoices;

I enjoy a monastic diet of bean soup and celery
—salt is the main constituent of my salary.
I never do anything and rarely go anywhere;
what else is there to do, living on fresh air?

It is to yourself then, Lady Moneybags, that I turn,
in the hope that forty years faithful service will earn
recognition at last, and if not wealth untold,
at least some small supplement for my billfold.

I have sacrificed lustful daydreams, grotesque fantasies
of handstitched lapels, silk shirts and a white Mercedes,
lace tablecloths all set about with lapis lazuli
candlesticks, and at every meal fine Chablis

in a Victorian wine glass with a hollow stem
—let those that truly appreciate such things have them.
I renounce all corrupt and bizarre thoughts of sex
on a sprung mattress padded with cashed cheques,

the ecstatic surrender of counterfoils and gilt
edged securities under a luxury quilt
of exchequer bonds, matured policies and the rest
not wishing to overheat a humble nest.

For nothing exotic matches what is said
plainly between loving friends in a firm, hard bed,
while supine comfort yawns and generates
languid ennui where true love suffocates.

A modest request, then, for some of your favours;
freshen me up, resuscitate me with a few fivers,
a Girocheque maybe, containing a tax rebate,
a small brass handshake embossed with today's date,

a lottery ticket with three matching devices
or the pools win that always remedies a crisis,
a sudden windfall from a passing lorry,
any sound credit note issued *To John Gohorry*

a premium bond, a change of heart in banks,
for any one of these, my heartfelt thanks.

For Breughel's Notebook

They brought her in at about seven in the evening,
the sun hanging low between Meindert and Oudskarpel
and the Meerwater ringing with fish rising to feed;

her long, dark hair matted with kelp and sea kale
had caught in their net webbing where mullet and bass
still thrashed and foundered, but she lay motionless
as the men reached into her beauty with salty hands
and guttural exclamations of wonder. Pieter Houyten,
known for a connoisseur of good wine and fine women,

finding that tapering fingers and exquisite manicure
proved her a Frenchwoman, whispered his little French
to her delicate drowned ear—*Quy v's ez bele, midons!*

—while poor Jan de Boek, their soft-headed handyman
from Pompmolen, blubbered helplessly *Ik verzoeke jou,
geliefd' Margaretha, kom uit'n de water,* thinking her
no doubt his beloved sister, vanished these dozen years.
She still lay as if stunned, bobbing amid other fish,
until Rijk van der Weyden swept his steel gutting knife

in an abrupt arc, shearing the tar-sealed seine-knots,
and then these men, knowing so much of fishes' recovery,
watched in amazement as she shook into her new freedom,

vanished at once into the complete privacy of the Meer.
Thankful, they hauled the lesser catch back to Oudskarpel
sharing already the doubts that they knew would be theirs
when they told for the third time how she had foundered
in their nets, as they stood by, rubbing their eyes,
pinching themselves, in the hope that it might be true.

On the Edge

Hogan, a footman, pulled her out of the early morning
water, the park being generally deserted, and himself
jilted the night before having thought of ending it all
in the same way, but reprieved. She floated towards him

unseasonable as a flowering lily in the December frost
which made the lake sparkle, her skirts spread wide,
their drenched fabric forming a rondel about her head.
He knew her for a respectable lady, her hands neatly

manicured and an expensive ring on her marriage finger;
it shone still. Then he saw under her heart the bunched
tumulus, put his hand hopelessly on the drowned satin.
He called out and the lake froze as they drew her away.

New Year's Day at Grafham Water

The first days of Creation were like this—the imagined
land scarcely formed between water and water, lake and sky
in a loud, hustling downpour, and darkness and light
still not agreeing their limits, but savaging one another

with the fury of novel hatreds. In this drenched universe
our memories clamour dispersedly—charred offcuts of wood
at the lake edge, a few birds drowned and dismembered
among the reed-blades, their throats already whispering

for the service of maggots, and under the leaden terrarium
at the centre, a naked, forked thing abseiling down a rope
to the pediment, beyond hope of mercy. He measures the
    wind,
the ooze-chapels below, suffocating under the thick silt,

and the spirals of cormorants, that skewer some guessed
    headland.
We keep to the perimeter wall, heads low in the turbulence,
our language a hailing deluge of bubbles and white froth.
In the condensing white sky a bird screams and a man
    drowns.

From Dunwich Cliffs

Under the bay, the drowned city remembers
while on the cliff walk tourists imagine:-
driving silt shifts through the archways
of chantry and Maison Dieu; human skulls

drop out of the cliff sands into the sea
like seabirds returning home. They nest
at the clifftop in All Saints churchyard,
their sleep undermined by ants sifting

bones all year long, the sea hungry too
for the cliff-base, its chosen foothold.
Burying them years ago in the fine sands,
they knew how the sea edged its way inland,

for their history was erosion, a stealthy
disappearance of chapels and market stalls,
but could not imagine that length of reach
over two centuries inching the very last

occupant of the gull's nest graveyard off
his perch and into the moon-washed shingle.
Then, John Brinkley Easey, may your fall be
a gentle one when the cold bay claims you,

and parading once more in those long drowned
streets may you remember again the old, dry
days, when you walked out over the far sea,
watched the high spires soaring into air.

The True Story of Francisco de la Vega

They came on him in their nets fishing out of Cadiz,
his eye cold as a pike's and his body grown over
with lampreys and barnacles, his green loins hissing
seaweed and crusty with salt as they lowered him gently

to the floor of their barge. After Brother Antoninus
had ascertained that he was a man, not a sea monster,
he spoke only once, pronouncing the word *Lierganes*,
the name, it was discovered from travellers' maps,

of a village five hundred miles off, by Santander Bay.
There Brother Antoninus escorted the wonderful manfish,
a prodigious, lone circus sideshow for one-horse towns,
but he would not speak to his mother, nor to the loud men

with smooth faces who called him Francisco, recalling
the sad day five years before when he dived into the Bahia
and never resurfaced. Nine years he remained with them,
never surfacing into speech, gazing up at the Cordilleras

at the back of the village, his loose scales flaking away,
and the web of his hands only comfortable in wet weather.
And then, one day, inspecting his face in a mirror,
he knew that cold eye for his eye, and himself for a fish;

slipped that very night into the waters, as fishermen left
on the high tide for the herring shoals out in far Biscay.
He was only seen once ever again, by Manuel Garrachuria
of La Cavada, our next village, who knew the family well,

and two years afterwards was travelling around the coast
to a cousin in Ortigueira. It was neither dolphin nor seal,
he was sure, that raised its intelligent head from the sea
off Cabo Moras, looked hard into his heart, and was gone.

An Incident in the Plaza del Zocodover, Toledo, 1584

The steel heat has withdrawn; magenta light flickers
   among the exact orangetrees, fading camellias,
   and the high, jetting fountains that irrigate

the park air to textures that are diffusely moist,
   fragrant and breatheable; mandolines flutter
   their languid vibrato upon the *barandillas*

marking the walkways, and San Miguel's diffident bell
   qualifies the gentle transition of a half-hour,
   calling the secular congregations to step out

in their fluorescent shirts for the evening promenade,
   the routine ostentation of finery that is also
   exchange of civilities, a dozen kept rendezvous,

the vivid clatter of gossip and freshly-told anecdote,
   the little displays that untangle collisions,
   perpetuate misunderstanding, and give our days

something short of coherence but spiralling nonetheless
   up towards it, like these vaulting cascades
   pitching high, and as they fall, spreading

their watery loveliness over the basinwork underneath
   where marble itself turns fluent, and carved
   stones engage one another in turbulent colloquy.

Now Señor Castellar in dark cloak and elegant sombrero
   escorts his diminutive wife to the fountain side
   in her lace shawl; the González family

parade formally down the avenues in dignified state
   like worshippers at the Fiesta de la Virgen.
   There are the Romeros, the Pérez, Ramírez;

one-eyed Dr Santos with symmetrically waxed moustaches
and silver-topped walking-cane; Señor Armado
discoursing on how the geraniums burst into flame

on the balcony of the Casa Dolores; Señor Alfonso Cobrán
with his grand-daughter, all pink ribbons
and ringlets, and Don Alberto de Falla,

the *corregidor's* clerk, who admires the wrought ironwork
of the park railings, a regular, black sonority
that lifts itself skywards at the ornate fluted arch

of each gateway. Lovers, too, keep their assignments
by the carefully-trimmed borders, and whisper
their gentle endearments beside the tulip beds

brimming with bees, whose foraging murmurs supply
a continuo to the urbane counterpoint
of the promenaders. Fabiano and Isabella

exchange a discreet kiss while admiring the fig trees
under the vigilant eye of her chaperone,
and the carp nosing like scarlet torpedoes

among the marine lilies; Juanita Pequeña caresses
her Tomaso's hand with restrained ardour
as the park-keeper's doves skirmish playfully

over their whitewashed dovecote, eddying feathers
and quilted calls. Time is a footstep
measuring paces upon the soused fountain

gravels, the oblique dance of sunlight winging its path
in a leafy *morisco* through the singing acacias,
and the cool breeze that has climbed the *meseta*

to freshen itself in the shadows behind the Alcázar,
while space has abandoned mere distances
to become an agenda of memory and desire

no further extended than mandoline strings, or the joined
   lips of united lovers. Now San Miguel el Alto
   announces three-quarters with his tin bell

and to the Portingale embassy on the far side of the square
   drive the gay coaches, doors bossed with flamboyant
   insignia, their delicate gilt hub-tracery

making the wheels flare with a sudden pulse as the ebony
   felloes churn and their steel rims ricochet
   sparks from the milled pavement. Footmen

perruked and liveried alight from their rails, opening
   carriage doors with a flourish of white gloves
   to discover interiors burning with red leather,

green baize, silk cushions for damasked arms, so that
   the occupants arriving for the *Baile de máscaras*
   are fabulous ornaments from some exotic *joyería,*

or meticulous clockwork figurines springing to animation
   when their lid is withdrawn. Here arrives
   Don Seguro, his coachman sporting a plumed

cockade, peacock's eyes iridescent against the hatband;
   Conde Cedillo and his Condesa descend, she
   in a white organdie gown hemmed with poppies;

extravagant Don José, his fists encrusted with sapphires,
   moves like a coral reef fanned by enraptured admirers
   to the dazzling marble steps. In the glass foyer

dancing with candlelight, Rafael de las Rocas discases
   himself to a whispering steward, as his Marquesa
   acknowledges Don Nabo, Ambassador to the Swedes,

with a gracious, slight inclination, and Conde Ampurias,
   Don Pedro de Alfaroubeira, who has seen the world,
   adjusts his lapel orchid in a stuccoed mirror.

Music spills out into the public air; the hubbub of voices
and snatches of sudden laughter traverse opened
windows, so that when Señor Armado observes

thankfully that they are witnessing some brilliant epiphany
his wife cannot tell whether he means the geraniums
or the bright celebrations within. Isabella, too,

her attention drawn from the pool to an imagined interior
never accessible to her, dreams of a scarlet dress,
and herself gliding gracefully among polite dancers

who trawl her with compliments not wholly ritual. Little
Stella Cobrán is already a white dove spiralling
to her invisible roost high on the balcony

where Conde Ampurias breaks his heart for a glass slipper
and her grandfather, court magician, transforms
the lapel orchid into his vanished bride

with one flick of a magic wand, and they dance together
joyfully over the parquet in a whirling quadrille
to his distant castle and happiness ever after.

From his shuttered apartment in the Calle de la Venganza
a man of early middle years joins the promenade;
he is quite alone, and, anonymous, might be taken

for some scholar walking abroad tonight to purge
        melancholy,
    or a contemplative setting out to devise soulful
    poesias to be written down after midnight when

the tenement sleeps—or perhaps, simply, this evening,
one who observes how the *lagartos* chase themselves
in and out of the lengthening shadowpatches

on the whitewashed wall of the barracks, themselves fugitive
shadows, it seems, yet agile as summer lightning.
His absorbed eyes proffer no acknowledgement;

51

he expects neither to greet nor receive greeting, but stalks
   the pathways unnoticed by knots of preoccupied citizens
   for whom Señor Promedio conjures no memory,

propagates no desire. He fingers the white scarf with a black
   silken border, that will serve for recognition,
   his mind turning fixedly on the anterior event

that has brought him to this pursuit—the boy hanging up
   in the orchard, eyes oozing like overripe damsons,
   his tongue an obscene blue fig in a red jar,

flies threading their paragraphs in and out of his nostrils
   like bees at some fragrant flower and the murderous
   Portingale who is the presumed hangman uttering

Senecan threats to the appletrees. He scans the
        thoroughfares,
   the pistols in each deep pocket knocking his thighs
   like fencing inexpertly vaulted; he cradles

their butts in his palms, which do not perspire, but balance
   in careful deliberation each smooth, coralled bullet
   that yearns like a lodestone for the true magnetic

north of the Senecan's heart, whence he imagines
        snakevenom
   pushing a fearful course along thickened arteries
   to a frozen, expressionless face. He will give him

a fatal and lead-sealed antidote, so that peonies
        unpredictably
   bloom in crimson extravagance before Señor Castellar
   or at the feet of the six discalced Carmelite

brothers trooping in formal lines out of their cedar grove,
   their white habits suggesting angelic cohorts
   or the candid purity of the park-keeper's doves.

Now San Miguel calls compline aloud in his high staccato,
   and at the promised hour steps the liveried
   Portingale to his pre-arranged rendezvous

with Señor Puntual, the Viceroy's gold badge at his collar
  enamelled, it seems, with his victim's blood;
  his eyes quarter the walkways to identify

a man with a black-edged neckscarf on undisclosed business
  who lies unsuspected among the nodding camellias
  drawn already upon his approaching quarry.

He squinies along the barrel, as Stella Cobrán spying one
  of the pious Brothers abandons her balcony
  and sprints over the lawn, arms outstretched,

calling joyfully to the barefoot giant for his embrace,
  straight into the firepath. Doves maul the air;
  the white dress collapses. *'Hark, gentlemen;*

this is a pistol shot,' shouts the captain of sentinels
  high on his brass horse at the barrack wall,
  and rowels his mount forward into the park.

Brother Juan cries in anguish, and merciful Dr Santos
  kneels by him at her side while the scattering
  crowd seethe with pity and terror; the Senecan,

alerted to danger, turns to flee, but the hidden marksman
  fires his second device at the enamelled badge
  whispering *'Allí quedó dormido'* as epitaph

to his toppling victim, who expires philosophically,
  for as Brother Juan blesses him, *'Fata si
  miseros iuvant,'* he gurgles, *'habes salutem;*

fata si vitam negant, habes sepulchrum.' In the embassy
  the dance music lifts itself to a crescendo,
  champagne corks fusillade upwards to the bodies

of naked cherubs; among the maskers, it is impossible
  to determine which derive satisfaction from
  paid accounts, for their pupils are enigmatic

—mere slits in the ecstasy of the dance and the violin
flurry that ravishes anonymities, sweeping
conspirators incognito over the chequered floor

in a whirling measure suggestive of carousels. Night
bursts like a tortured volcano over Gethsemane
and the fugitive citizens extinguish themselves

one by one from the square, as the butcher is apprehended
and hauled off, away to the damp barrack flagstones
for summary execution. The embassy guests, too,

practise desertions, passing down through the bevelled foyer
and off in the torchflare of their midnight coaches
to their beds and their indiscretions. Silence

quickens in an efflorescence of cypress and numinous cloud,
the great city, silver and green, losing its substance
in a vortex of grief and fear, as pity implores

the infirmary hourglass with a *'Be still, sands of time,
be still, let her be still.'* But the sands collapse
downwards inexorably into their white tumuli

and punctual clocks measure the dreadful nightspaces out
at accustomed intervals—*las cuatro, las cinco
y cuarto, y media*, bells tolling the daylight in

until a terrible, raw sky recreates the Alcantára Bridge
and the summit of Hannequin's tower in its vivid
flame, the Conde Ampurias leaves a dissolved dream

for the desolate rituals of his dressing-mirror, ashen-faced
at a withered orchid, and doves summoned down out
of starlight for better beginnings than this murmur

*'Vrecrou, crou, crou—pierce our hearts, Prince of the Morning,
with your bright blade, for how shall we ever fly
over the cedars again, our Beloved now turned to stone?'*

The Therapists

In the last century they might have been novelists
—the fortnightly serial culminating in a three-decker
worked over, against the clock, on long afternoons—
or perhaps mere hack bodgers of prose by the quire,
filching obscure paragraphs from the *Gentleman's Magazine*
or the *Lady's Portmanteau*, turning a hard coin
at the quill's end. Either way, these compiled

their serious, sustained fictions, the bay window
giving onto the Park Pastures, or Grub Street tumbling
through its ant-heap errands always pulling the eye
away from the smudged page, inviting corrections,
or, even, a short walk. But the therapists spin
their endless, plausible fictions in a great cavern
of mirrors; and should we, their invention,

after our regular group want to make body-trespass,
we find their contrived landscapes too formal to be
either authentic, or comfortable in—these pillows
are mere catalysts for aggression. Being fabulous
in this setting, we are subject only to such
revisions as will sustain it—vainly dream of
the street, the park spaces where we were once real.

Magic Stall Clignancourt, 1979

Words here take on new surfaces. Between a *quincaillerie*
suggestive of cans clattering, of clanking, and can-cans,
and a candle-stall under whose dark celestial tarpaulins
a modern Ronsard might sing by the clear light of the moon
... *Quand vous serez bien vieille, au soir, à la chandelle* ...
is the factual daylight logic of Chiquello's magic stall.

Everything's here that the wondering heart could wish for
—tarot packs, magic handkerchieves, boxes full of illusion
(top hats, impossible yards of bunting, vanishing doves)
—mirrors that throw back the heart's embryonic imaginings
to the beholder's amazed eye as substantial as life itself;
a perpetual *natura naturans* that transforms Clignancourt

to pure calembour in a twinkling—*un clin d'oeuil court.*
The Prince of the Abracadabras observes everything
    carefully
through thick black-framed spectacles which have no lenses;
his Golems grotesquely posed on the red gingham tablecloth
beside clockwork Coppelias and Houdin's automata,
    homunculi
in an arrested stasis that requires only a pass of the hand

and a hey presto! to bring them to life again. A neat card
propped at Coppelia's foot reads *Prière de ne pas toucher.*
What tense could be right to disclose these particulars in
at a distance of five hundred miles and almost a decade?
Brasshead spoke only three times, then collapsed into pulver,
past, present and future sucked into their common interior.

My substance was not hid from thee when I was made in secret
prayed the vanishing bishop; was memory afterwards
    deceived
as at present these eyes by a juggling pack of cards? *Valet,
Dame; voilà, madame!* the handkerchief scurries into a sleeve
and the dove flutters up and away into the grey overcast sky
of the February imagination. The illusion is real, tangible.

Terra Damnata

Subtle: Take away the recipient,
            And rectify your menstrue from the *phlegma*.
            Then pour it o' the Sol, in the *cucurbite*,
            And let 'em macerate together.
Face: Yes, sir.
            And save the ground?
Subtle: No. *Terra damnata*
            Must not have entrance in the work.

— Ben Jonson *The Alchemist* II v

1. ILLUC

The cliffs drop astern of our charted merchanter,
ever less hiant as distance relinquishes them

to the low horizon, our killock up at the cathead
and the catastrums apert to fair weather. Already

we have passed Sillabar and the Insulae Angustae,
the Straits of Annian, the Greater & Lesser Tondas,

and our business is faking cables, securing timenoguys,
and watching the jolly trail lazily from the guesswarps.

Now we sight Maelsuyker, and, further south, Nuyts Land
which some call Terra Damnata, our destinied landing stage;

the dogwatches pocket their scrimshaw, call for incolers.
We debouch, our fresh ketehood stubborn as medrinacks.

2. A REAL OLD COUNTRY DANCE

The Fenchmore Leadman has been drinking juter,
his duddels thrown off, the capriny hastard;

even the journ-chopper, pornial in this colligence,
waves his gannok about, crampland amid his ounds.

All that theaming momblishness of The Coysell
as he took thitling from the Curriedows!

Where is our rip-towel? they ask, *what has
that cowdrice galverly brought off this time?*

He rides off in the jimwhiskee, his cluttish
shairl reeking of owser, weasy as ever.

3. A SEASONAL LAMENT

She lay all in teen by the wilger tree
—twangdillow, twangdillow, what does she vizy?

her prew Dametas now all turned gullion,
the faithless swingebreech, gone with another.

That scowbanker enamorato with his flim-flam villanellas
made love out of shuffs merely, poor kickshiwinshes;

she weighs love on the ansellshaft, and her heart is heavy.
Weariness now is her shotclog, sorrow her dole.

4. ROUGH JUSTICE FOR WATER THIEVES

The guest-taker and all his old cookmates boarded
the Dutch bullenger moored at Ouster-le-Mer

freighted with sacratyle partels, the gyronetty
showing a steady south easterly, and would have made

minovery there, selling them off to the macegriefs;
but suddenly there comes the late evening tranect

across the estuary, the Tinemen hardly visible
and the Tantlings not at all in the thick darkness.

Some unauthorised sound, ennoisies, proleptic of gain,
sets our Captain to play tip-cheese with those pardeluns;

there is a pavade struggle, brief, bloody, and decisive.
The Mistress will have cone and key, and her new filours

5. A FASHIONABLE PAIR

Here's Sharnbud, a privisant, tall man, her sweetakin,
sporting his brand new drabdrubbery and silk famblers,

and on his arm Spigurnel all lah-di-dah farthingale
and mantled fontanges, a proper nicebecetur.

The clapperdudgeons bait them in envious scoggery
—call him true prickmedainty, mamuque, popingoe,

and her marsheet, pompardy-monger, simper-de-cocket.
But they pass by, heads erect, girned by such tediouste.

6. A ROADSIDE ENTERTAINMENT

Their mother being due for the next birthing,
the eme takes his patruels off for a long shanksmarch

until musha! hey presto! there's the Qualtagh
raring up handy-dandy out of the queaches,

all comethers and calembours for his high rigmarolery.
He gives them some grand fallings and five cartwheels,

whisks conies out of the grego and endless silk torchons
but then comes the Harman in a great thode

and glares at him skenningly. They give him gliciride
for his quitshilling, their best quality relevavith.

He avoids, gratefully, back to morels and runches.
They go home marvelling, eager for blithemeat.

7. FROM THE SICILIAN MUSE

Preposterously they pass through the hedgerow in gauche
  murlimews
to the shippen, cagastrical Magi for the newly-born Princeps
  Mundi,

first Snaphaunce, the fixnet gegge, robed in grey
  musterdevillers,
his saddlebags farcied with Mannheim gold and heaped
  chadfarthings,

then Goinfre, his males wrung with nith, lugging plucked
  whaups
and a fine goibert bloodripe for the skillet, then Nekard
  third,

with his handsel of jessamy and dark Venice Treacle, specific
against chincough and quinsy. Not susquedeques these,
  prostrating

themselves low under the thick lintel, nor hixius-doxius
    quaegemes,
but honoured guests, his guests of honour. The hot-breathed
    mounsel

squiny around them as the shabroons shog off their great
    fardels.
The Parviculate cognises his Gammerstang with a gay smile.

8. DR QUINCUNX ADVISES

The heart wearing exuccous, there is great innitency
about it, hypomochlion one way to the fougades

of all cremable nature, and the other to verticities
of emphatical diuturnity, solisequious *ubi*

where love is charted in Archidoxis and Targum.
Therefore bring castle-soap, the crasis of all *utinams,*

and, that neither venny nor incrassation of Time
turn all this gravelled flax over to the vespilloes,

let him keep it moist with *quaere* and sad conjecture,
inundating clamations, oneirocritical glomes,

and when knowledge should seem to lose compage of parts,
always a new word, flosculous, nutritive as secondine.

9. A CHILIAST LOOKS TO THE FUTURE

In the frumshaft was there nobbut Drighten
and his dighel rede working, his dark freols;

then were all our yomering and our mandreams
fast in his breastwork, until in the middantide

he made spell all brimfowl, all Geshaft matheling
its drycraft of kennings, tongues wurthen ythes,

ethel of whales, loud with heryings. O Shippend
that in the tocume-time wrixles all to thy weird,

be that first Word still and ever our every ward;
that frumshaft unfathomed ever, even in ferndays.

10. TERRA DAMNATA

What country should this be, where Ettin and Ehequehere
hinny about a kewaw world quoined utterly mixtermaxter

in their Mahagonny wordframe, the nuchthemerinal
    experiment
already in fat-time, and nothing but *caput mortuum* still

keelivined from the wordblocks? Pomelio dreams of those
    balgh
Lisbon mares that conceive by the wind, their foals always

still-born of hypenemies, as the blocks tumble and turn
a poesis of floccinaucities, mere sooterkins, nothing celse.

But then by miracle their conjoined dreams move to
    juncture,
their bright Xanaduvian tryptych scintillant as a nimbus;

the *logos* glows like a shekinah in brand-new chantepleures
—they rehearse them, in whispers, for the conceived Ieros.

11. ILLIC

Bawncocher main, saddeens odrone conaty lilamon,
quall farpleysher adreynte ey so tan tamany?

Cother larn saradell, cother born feyrnfre anatill?
Draygeth porther, fallawn min; cothero mantany.

Quallo *ag, tasho, drem, cushdo, danity:*
quallesto *vec, mago, fronsel, rannaces, danity.*

Saddens conaty, barncocher min, saddenzie ayn fransanill;
heigh, heigh, tans a deir ayny lantel gahoun!

Quallo born saradell, aththe a larn sentany!
Quallo porther fallawn, fallawn min cothero mantany.

Quallo *ag, tasho, drem, cushdo, danity:*
quallesto *vec, mago, fronsel, rannaces, danity.*